Waiting

Dail
Adve

Robert F. Morneau

LITURGICAL PRESS

Collegeville, Minnesota

www.litpress.org

Nihil Obstat: Reverend Robert Harren, *Censor deputatus.*
Imprimatur: ✚ Most Reverend Donald J. Kettler, J.C.L., Bishop of
Saint Cloud, Minnesota. March 20, 2014.

Cover design by Ann Blattner. Photo: Thinkstock by Getty Images.

ISSN: 1550-803X
ISBN: 978-0-8146-3560-5   978-0-8146-3585-8   (ebook)

Introduction

Some of us may remember the first day of school: a new book bag, pencils sharpened, reunion of classmates, anticipation of new knowledge! Even though summer leisure was gone, new opportunities arose for our enrichment.

Advent is a new beginning. With the universal church, we are invited to prepare our minds and hearts to celebrate the Christmas mysteries. Rich opportunities will be ours to welcome Jesus more deeply into our lives, be it through the pondering of Scripture, reaching out to the needy, or celebrating the sacraments week after week. Hopefully, our enthusiasm will be sustained better than in our school days. Hopefully, each day will offer us the opportunity to grow in wisdom and love.

Just over fifty years ago the Second Vatican Council commenced. After three years of hard work and dedication, sixteen documents were promulgated, providing us a vision of the church and a call to further God's kingdom. That council was a type of "advent," a time of both renewal and conversion. Here are several themes from the council that we might ponder this Advent season.

"The church, in Christ, is a sacrament—a sign and instrument, that is, of communion with God and of the unity of the entire human race" (Dogmatic Constitution on the Church 1). Our focus in Advent is on the person of Jesus who came to restore unity (i.e., redemption). Jesus' prayer is that all may be one, one with the Father and one community. There is no better way to live out our Advent than by being an instrument of that union and unity. We do that by prayer, service, and sharing.

The church's "duty . . . is to foster and elevate all that is true, all that is good, and all that is beautiful in the human community" (Pastoral Constitution on the Church in the Modern World 76). Advent has a job description. It is a season of pondering the truth revealed in Jesus' incarnation, doing what is good by helping others, and appreciating the beauty of the human person and creation. During these four weeks, our work is cut out for us as we take on the agency of making the transcendentals—truth, goodness, beauty—real in the life of the church and world.

"For the liturgy, through which 'the work of our redemption takes place,' especially in the divine sacrifice of the Eucharist, is supremely effective in enabling the faithful to express in their lives and portray to others the mystery of Christ and the real nature of the true church" (Constitution on the Sacred Liturgy 2). In this Advent season we focus on Jesus and the community he came to establish. It is in celebrating the Mass that we give thanks for the mysteries of creation, redemption, and our sanctification. In word and sacrament we come to know who we are and what we are to do. The Eucharist offers us the grace to be authentic disciples.

In his opening address inaugurating the Second Vatican Council, Pope John XXIII stated, "In this assembly, under the guidance of the Holy Spirit, we wish to inquire how we ought to renew ourselves, so that we may be found increasingly faithful to the Gospel of Christ" (Message to Humanity). Is this not also the purpose of our Advent season?

FIRST WEEK OF ADVENT

November 30: First Sunday of Advent

Living in Expectation

Readings: Isa 63:16b-17, 19b; 64:2-7; 1 Cor 1:3-9;
Mark 13:33-37

Scripture:
No ear has ever heard, no eye ever seen, any God but you
    doing such deeds for those who wait for him. (Isa 64:3b)

Reflection: The Irish playwright Samuel Beckett (1906–89)
wrote *Waiting for Godot*, a play in which two characters wait
in vain for anything to happen. Simone Weil (1909–43) had
friends who put together some of her thoughts and entitled
the work *Waiting for God*. If there is a single theme that stands
out for us during Advent, indeed, that stands out in all of
life, it is the theme of waiting, of living in expectation.

In *Waiting for Godot* the two characters, Vladimir and
Estragon, spoke without hope. In *Waiting for God* we find a
real-life pilgrim who struggled in the darkness and yet lived
with a faith that offered hope. That hope was experienced
in the gifts of friendship that God sent her way. Simone Weil
found traces of God in her search for truth and justice. Her
waiting was not in vain. Her mystical experience in praying
George Herbert's poem "Love III" confirmed, once and for
all, that God does come to those who stand and wait.

Two major components of waiting are being watchful and
being alert. Jesus is emphatic in the gospel: "Be watchful! Be

alert! . . . Watch! (Mark 13:33a, 37b). Advent waiting is not a passive matter but one of intense urgency. We can almost hear the words: "Code Blue! Code Blue!" Something is happening. God is already near if we have eyes to see and ears to hear. One is reminded of Aslan the lion in C. S. Lewis's *The Chronicles of Narnia*. When least expected, Christ comes to us.

Saint Paul experienced the revelation of God in Jesus. As he writes to the Corinthians in today's second reading he reminds them that they have been given spiritual gifts "as you wait for the revelation of our Lord Jesus Christ" (1 Cor 1:7b). Paul knew the fidelity of God and confirmed that faithfulness by telling the community to stand firm.

Meditation: What is your experience of waiting, waiting for a baby to arrive, waiting for reconciliation, waiting for a spiritual consolation? What is the connection between waiting and being alert? Are your expectations of God, of life, of yourself realistic?

Prayer: Gracious and faithful God, give us the grace to wait and watch; give us the grace of faith to trust that you are near, here and now. When our days are dark and our hearts are empty, send an angel to point the way. Our waiting ends with your arrival in word and sacrament or in another person.

December 1: Monday of the First Week of Advent

War and Peace

Readings: Isa 2:1-5; Matt 8:5-11

Scripture:
One nation shall not raise the sword against another,
  nor shall they train for war again. (Isa 2:4b)

Reflection: On October 4, 1965, while the last session of the Second Vatican Council was underway, Pope Paul VI went to the United Nations to address this international organization. The pope spoke eloquently of the need for peace and about the horrors of war. Then he cried out, "No more war! War never again! It is peace, peace that must guide the destiny of the peoples of the world and of all humanity" (Address to United Nations General Assembly).

During this season of Advent we await the Prince of Peace, our Lord Jesus. In celebrating his birth we also remember his death and resurrection. In one of Jesus' appearances after the resurrection he bestowed on the frightened disciples the gift of peace. "Peace be with you. . . . Receive the holy Spirit" (John 20:21-22).

Ironically, the centurion in the gospel, one trained for war, comes to Jesus and receives the gift of peace through the healing of the centurion's son. One might wonder if after this miraculous event the centurion changed his profession. Even if he didn't, surely his life took on a new tone of compassion and gratitude because of his encounter with Jesus.

Swords and spears! Plowshares and pruning hooks! The same metal put to different uses. God has given to individuals and nations tremendous energy and freedom. How those gifts will be channeled and used depends upon human choice. Will it be war or peace? Will we ever learn to live as members of the same human family with God as our Father?

Meditation: As you read history, why do wars predominate? By contrast, when you read the lives of the saints, why do these individuals merit our emulation?

Prayer: Providential God, give us the grace to be instruments of your peace. Help us to be reconciled to one another and to live with mutual respect. May wars come to an end; may peace reign in our hearts and in our world. Jesus, Prince of Peace, empower us to follow in your way.

December 2: Tuesday of the First Week of Advent

The Prophet's Band and Belt

Readings: Isa 11:1-10; Luke 10:21-24

Scripture:
Justice shall be the band around his waist,
  and faithfulness a belt upon his hips. (Isa 11:5)

Reflection: Isaiah and Jesus were prophets. As such they lived out the graces of justice and fidelity.

Isaiah, in one of the most eloquent passages of the Old Testament, describes a world in which peace reigns and all experience the glory of the Lord. Someone is coming who is filled with God's Spirit; someone is coming who will restore the unity lost by sin. Not only will human relationships be made whole, but even in the animal world, there will be a startling peace. Of course, this stump and root of Jesse is none other than Jesus.

Jesus is *the* prophet. Rejoicing in the Holy Spirit, Jesus offers praise and thanksgiving to the Father for the gift of revelation, the manifestation of love and mercy that the childlike, and not the wise, appreciate. Jesus calls the disciples truly blessed in that they hear and see God's love made manifest in his very person.

Jesus reveals the justice of God, a God who is deeply concerned about right relationships. Thus gifts are given—wisdom and understanding, counsel and strength, knowledge and fear of the Lord—all to help us to build the kingdom. Through baptism we are called to do the works of justice, promoting and protecting the rights of all. If we have this band around our waist, we are authentic disciples.

Jesus was faithful; Jesus did the will of his Father. Everything was handed over to the Son and the Son cherished and nurtured the gifts of life and love. As disciples we too are called to faithfulness, to discern and do God's will. If the belt of faithfulness is upon our hips, we are truly good stewards.

Meditation: In what ways do you demonstrate a life of justice and faithfulness? As Advent people, what can we do to make the world more just? How can we live out the call to fidelity more fully?

Prayer: Lord Jesus, you revealed to your disciples the mystery of your Father's love and mercy. Help us to have eyes to see your presence; help us to have ears to hear your daily call. Make us a just and faithful people through the gift of your Holy Spirit. Come, Lord Jesus, come.

December 3:
Saint Francis Xavier, Priest (Catholic Church)
Wednesday of the First Week of Advent (Episcopal Church)

On the Mountain

Readings: Isa 25:6-10a; Matt 15:29-37

Scripture:
At that time:
Jesus walked by the Sea of Galilee,
   went up on the mountain, and sat down there. (Matt 15:29)

Reflection: Back in 1980, Alan Paton (1903–88), the South African reformer and novelist, wrote an autobiographical work, *Towards the Mountain*. Paton talks about his "journey to that holy mountain, where they do not hurt or destroy." In today's readings we hear about "the mountain," the one that Jesus climbed and then encountered the crowds, the one that Isaiah tells of where the food is rich and the wine is pure. On God's mountain there is no hurt or destruction. On God's mountain there is healing and enhancement of life.

On the mountain a message is given: tears will be wiped away, death itself will be destroyed, the web and veil that hinder encounter will be removed. On God's mountain, juicy food and choice wines are freely given. On this holy place we behold the God who saves and forgives us.

On the mountain Jesus heals the lame and the blind, the deformed and the mute. On the mountain, Jesus, out of deep compassion, provides food for the body, so much so that the crowds "ate and were satisfied." So abundant was this eucharistic miracle that the leftovers filled seven baskets.

During these dark days of Advent, we walk in the valley toward the mountain. We experience tears and hurt and hunger. We long for healing but are so conscious of our brokenness. We seek to look upon the God of love and mercy revealed in Jesus and struggle with doubts and darkness. As a pilgrim people moving toward the mountain we are called to share our bread with the hungry and to commit ourselves to doing good and not to harm.

With the psalmist we pray, "I shall live in the house of the Lord all the days of my life" (Ps 23:6cd). In the house on the mountain God will give us peace and joy.

Meditation: What does the mountain symbolize for you? With whom do you travel as you head toward God's mountain? What obstacles do you encounter on your journey?

Prayer: Gracious God, draw us into your presence. We know of so much hurt and destruction. Send your Spirit of peace and justice into our world so that all peoples and nations might experience your healing touch and the richness of your divine banquet.

December 4: Thursday of the First Week of Advent
Saint John of Damascus, Priest and Doctor of the Church

Wisdom and Courage

Readings: Isa 26:1-6; Matt 7:21, 24-27

Scripture:
Jesus said to his disciples:
"Not everyone who says to me, 'Lord, Lord,'
    will enter the Kingdom of heaven,
    but only the one who does the will of my Father in
        heaven." (Matt 7:21)

Reflection: Saint John of Damascus (d. 749) strove to do the will of God as a Syrian monk and priest. As a composer of hymns and a defender of icons, this doctor of the church built his house on the rock foundation of Christ. His discipleship was not just one of prayer—"Lord, Lord"—but one of action as he fulfilled his baptismal call to be an evangelist.

We too, as an Advent people, are called to put our faith into action. Trusting in the Lord as our eternal rock, we venture forth in an ambiguous world to be agents of God's life and love. There will be obstacles: the rain of skepticism, the flood waters of materialism, the high wind of hedonism. Unless we have put our trust in Christ's indwelling Spirit, our houses and our lives will come tumbling down. Our wisdom will be manifest to the extent that God's will reigns in our minds and hearts.

Norman Cousins (d. 1990), political journalist, teacher, and peace advocate, was editor-in-chief of *Saturday Review* for thirty years. He had this to say about wisdom: "Wisdom consists of the anticipation of consequences." By contrast, fools fail because of their inability to foresee the effects of their choices. Jesus uses the metaphor of the foundation of a house to contrast wisdom and foolishness. Only those who listen and obey demonstrate a wise, courageous heart; those who hear but do not act face ruin.

In our gospel acclamation we have a piece of Advent wisdom: "Seek the LORD while he may be found; / call him while he is near" (Isa 55:6).

Meditation: Upon what or whom have you built your spiritual life? Is the anticipation of consequences all that difficult? Who are the wisdom figures in your life?

Prayer: Wise and merciful God, teach us to know what really matters on this journey of life. Too often we construct our hopes and dreams on cotton candy. Too often we purchase sand and not rock. Grant us the gifts of wisdom and courage so that we might discern and do your will.

December 5: Friday of the First Week of Advent

Evangelization: Spreading the Word

Readings: Isa 29:17-24; Matt 9:27-31

Scripture:
Jesus warned them [the healed blind men] sternly,
    "See that no one knows about this."
But they went out and spread word of him through all that
    land. (Matt 9:30b-31)

Reflection: How difficult it is to keep from telling good news, the good news of employment, the good news of successful surgery, the good news of God's healing love. Those of us who have had cataract surgery proclaim to our friends what a joy it is to see with clarity the radiance of the sun and the beauty of nature. How much more when blindness is removed, when deafness is healed, how much more when we are the object of God's redemptive love.

Jesus asked the blind men and he asks us a defining question: "Do you believe that I can do this?" (Matt 9:28b). Do what? Heal? Reconcile relationship? Bring peace to warring nations? Forgive sins? Through God's grace the two blind men cried out their exalted "Yes," at which point Jesus did what their faith desired. Jesus, the son of David, had pity on them and granted their request.

Advent darkness hungers for the light. We all want to see the glory of God; we all long for the vision of truth. It is faith that empowers us to trust in God's abiding presence even though our feelings and our daily experiences seem to say otherwise. If our faith is deep in spite of our intellectual struggles, we too will venture out to fulfill our baptismal duty of evangelization, spreading the word about *the* Word, Jesus, who is our Savior, brother, and friend.

In one of her letters Flannery O'Connor wrote, "Don't expect faith to clear things up for you. It is trust, not certainty . . ." The two blind men trusted Jesus and they were not disappointed.

Meditation: What is your description of faith? Do you consider evangelization to be part of your Christian discipleship? In what ways can we spread the good news of Jesus?

Prayer: Gracious God, heal our blindness so that we might see the mystery of your love and forgiveness. Give us the courage to share the good news of your Son Jesus with others, by word, by example, by personal contact. Deepen our faith in your everlasting love and mercy.

December 6: Saturday of the First Week of Advent

Saint Nicholas, Bishop (optional)

Troubled and Abandoned

Readings: Isa 30:19-21, 23-26; Matt 9:35–10:1, 5a, 6-8

Scripture:
At the sight of the crowds, his [Jesus'] heart was moved
    with pity for them
  because they were troubled and abandoned,
  like sheep without a shepherd. (Matt 9:36)

Reflection: Many of us have heard Louis Armstrong's rendition of the spiritual "Nobody knows the trouble I've seen / Nobody knows my sorrow." The song expresses in plaintive sounds the anguish of the human heart, the darkness of the human condition.

But then maybe, just maybe, Somebody does know the trouble and the sorrow of humanity. Maybe, just maybe, the God who created us came to live among us to experience from the inside what we go through on this perilous journey. Maybe, just maybe, the teaching, proclaiming, and healing of Jesus reveals God's infinite compassion.

And maybe, just maybe each one of us is called to participate in this divine compassion by being sent to the lost and the least. Saint Frances Xavier Cabrini (1850–1917) heard God's call and she and her community (Missionary Sisters of the Sacred Heart) reached out to the troubled and the abandoned, to those who lived in darkness and fear. By the time of her death in 1917, St. Frances and her community built and ran sixty-seven institutions (hospitals, orphanages, schools). As the patroness of immigrants and migrants, St. Frances continues to intercede for those sheep without a shepherd.

Jim Wallis offers a word of wisdom: "Proximity to poor people is crucial to our capacity for compassion" (*The Call to Conversion*). Proximity to the troubled and abandoned means we are in territory that Jesus traveled.

Meditation: When you were troubled or abandoned, who reached out to you? In what sense are we called to cure the sick, raise up the dead, cleanse lepers, and drive out demons? Where is this happening in the world today?

Prayer: Compassionate Jesus, plant your affection and courage in our hearts. May we truly feel compassion for all those who are lost and abandoned, troubled and afraid. Empower us to be agents of your kingdom and instruments of your peace.

SECOND WEEK OF ADVENT

December 7: Second Sunday of Advent

Ongoing Baptism

Readings: Isa 40:1-5, 9-11; 2 Pet 3:8-14; Mark 1:1-8

Scripture:
People of the whole Judean countryside
    and all the inhabitants of Jerusalem
    were going out to him [John the Baptist]
    and were being baptized by him in the Jordan River
    as they acknowledged their sins. (Mark 1:5)

Reflection: In the ritual of baptism, the symbols of water, oil, a white garment, and a candle express various aspects of this moment of grace. Water symbolizes life; the sacred chrism tells of anointing and consecration; the white garment is our being clothed in Christ, putting on his mind and heart; and the candle calls us to be light to the world and to share in the mission of Jesus who scattered the darkness of ignorance and sin.

When John the Baptist performed his ministry of baptism, he too took water and called the people of Jerusalem and all of Judea to repent and turn back to the Lord. John the Baptist was the chosen, anointed one, blazing the trail for his cousin Jesus. The courageous prophet was a light, shining brightly in a dark world. And this child of Zechariah and Elizabeth knew his origins and that one mightier than he would baptize with the Holy Spirit.

During this season of Advent, we continue to live out our baptismal callings, the call to holiness and service, the call to maturity and generosity. Though we were baptized in a specific moment in time and place, we are "being baptized" day in and day out as we are challenged to live the life of discipleship. The writer Jean Sulivan in his *Eternity, My Beloved* has this interesting phrase: "a vocation is given every morning." John the Baptist and Jesus himself lived out their vocation every morning.

Isaiah's prophetic vocation, like our own, was one of being an agent of God's love. He fulfilled his calling by being a messenger of God's vision, a vision wherein God feeds, gathers, carries, and leads all of us to our homeland. Isaiah, like John the Baptist, addressed the issue of sin and guilt. Isaiah baptized with words just as John baptized with water. Jesus, *the* prophet, would baptize with the Holy Spirit.

Meditation: What is your understanding of baptism? In what sense are we given a vocation every morning? Which of the baptismal calls—holiness, service, maturity, generosity—is claiming your attention this Advent?

Prayer: God of love and mercy, renew our baptism once again. Plunge us into the grace of your light and life. Forgive the sins we have committed; take away our guilt and shame. Morning after morning may we hear your call to discipleship. Help us to be light to the world, salt of the earth.

December 8: The Solemnity of the Immaculate Conception
(Catholic Church)

Monday of the Second Week of Advent (Episcopal Church)

Mary:
The Obedient, Humble, *and* Joyous One

Readings: Gen 3:9-15, 20; Eph 1:3-6, 11-12; Luke 1:26-38

Scripture:
Mary said, "Behold, I am the handmaid of the Lord.
May it be done to me according to your word."
Then the angel departed from her. (Luke 1:38)

Reflection: Was Thomas Merton correct in maintaining that obedience and humility contain the whole of the spiritual life? Such might be the case and we have in Mary, the mother of Jesus, someone who did what God asked of her (obedience) and someone who lived in the truth of things (humility).

But this obedience was not without its struggles. Mary had to wrestle with two elements of the human condition that challenge us all: fear and ignorance! Mary experienced trepidation in her encounter with God's messenger; Mary knew the terror of not knowing, aware, however, that something momentous was in the air. Deep down Mary trusted and this led to her obedient faith. Indeed, all is possible for those who believe *and* obey.

Humility, a virtue grounded in authentic self-knowledge, is an endangered species. Illusions and delusions abound in our human psyche, making it difficult to come to terms with our creatureliness. Mary accepted her identity: she was God's handmaid and placed her life in God's hand. Like her son Jesus, it was the Father's will that determined the direction of her life.

But surely there is something more to the interior life than just obedience and humility. Is there not a deep joy that shines in the annunciation story that transcends the fear and not knowing? It is the joy in the rightness of things, in the sinlessness of Mary's heart, in the incredible mystery of God taking on our humanity. The departing angel left with not only joy in a mission accomplished, but with a sense that peace, the Prince of Peace, now dwelt on earth.

Meditation: What ingredients of the spiritual life are most important to you? Do you see the grace of joy and peace in the annunciation story? Have any angels entered your life asking for obedience?

Prayer: Mary, pray that we emulate your obedient faith and joyful humility. Too often we fail to hear God's call; too often we allow pride and arrogance to govern our lives. Tell us to follow your example of doing God's will. May we, like you, say "yes" to whatever the Father asks of us.

All You Have to Know

Readings: Isa 40:1-11; Matt 18:12-14

Scripture:
Like a shepherd he [God] feeds his flock;
  in his arms he gathers the lambs,
Carrying them in his bosom,
  and leading the ewes with care. (Isa 40:11)

Reflection: The story is told of a second-grade teacher who believed in memorization. She worked diligently with her twenty students, especially in having them learn by heart their prayers and passages from Scripture. A big challenge: memorize Psalm 23. After weeks of work, the day for recitation came. Little Jimmy got up and began: "The Lord [pause] is [longer pause] my shepherd [silence]." His mind went blank and as he sat down he muttered, "That's all you have to know."

Could it be that Jimmy was right? Maybe all we have to know is that God is our shepherd, feeding, gathering, carrying, and leading all of us on the journey of life. And if there is any doubt here, Jesus came as the good shepherd who will leave the ninety-nine and go in search of anyone who is lost or who has strayed. God does pursue us "down the nights and down the days," as the poet Francis Thompson believed. And, of course, all one hundred sheep stand in need of redemption, such being the human condition.

In his study of Jesus, the theologian Romano Guardini writes, "The whole purpose of Jesus' life is to replace our human conceptions of God; not only the primitive, grotesque, but also the highest, purest and most refined." Philosophers have spoken of God as "First Cause." Theologians tell us that God is the "Ground of our Being" or "Ultimate Truth." Jesus shows us who God is by his compassionate, forgiving, and loving way of life. God is the good shepherd made present and manifest in Jesus.

Meditation: How has your image of God changed over the years? In what sense is God a good shepherd to you and your family?

Prayer: Jesus, you are our brother and friend, our Lord and Redeemer, our good shepherd. If we truly know and believe this, we will put greater reliance on your saving grace. You know our weakness. We all stray. When we are lost, please search us out and bring us back home.

December 10: Wednesday of the Second Week of Advent

A Non-Meticulous God

Readings: Isa 40:25-31; Matt 11:28-30

Scripture:
Jesus said to the crowds:
"Come to me, all you who labor and are burdened,
   and I will give you rest." (Matt 11:28)

Reflection: In our responsorial psalm for today's Mass we hear about the qualities of God: "Merciful and gracious is the LORD, / slow to anger and abounding in kindness. / Not according to our sins does he deal with us, / nor does he requite us according to our crimes" (Ps 103:8, 10). This is the God revealed in Jesus who invites all those who are weary from work or sin to come and find peace and rest. Why would we not hurry to a God who is merciful, gracious, and kind?

Yet we hesitate. George Herbert, in his poem "Love III," tells of his hesitancy to enter God's tent because of sin, especially the sin of ingratitude. Rather than focusing on a merciful God the poet turns in on himself (Augustine describes sin as *curvatus in se*—a turning in on oneself) and becomes paralyzed. God tells the versifier to look at the one who bore the weight of our sins. If we do that, we will experience the grace of freedom and enter God's presence.

Isaiah gives us additional qualities of God: God's knowledge is inscrutable, God does not faint or grow weary, God renews our strength, God is eternal and the creator of all life. During this Advent season we have a golden opportunity to learn more and more about the mystery of God through the prophets, the psalmist, the New Testament writers. If we "come" to this great resource, our burdens will be lightened and our labor eased. We may even experience the peace that is, as St. Paul tells us, beyond all understanding.

It might be of value to remember what St. Teresa of Avila said about God: "My God is not in the least meticulous." Such a God should be no threat to our messy human condition, to the burdens and sin we carry.

Meditation: What are the burdens that you carry? Who helps you to carry yours, and whom do you help in carrying theirs? Is your God meticulous or not?

Prayer: Gracious and merciful God, our trials and burdens are many. In our weariness, give us strength. In our discouragement, give us hope. In our fear, give us trust. Deepen our knowledge and love of you and free us from gazing too much at ourselves. Come, Lord Jesus, come.

December 11: Thursday of the Second Week of Advent

Great, Greater, Greatest

Readings: Isa 41:13-20; Matt 11:11-15

Scripture:
"Amen, I say to you,
   among those born of women
   there has been none greater than John the Baptist;
   yet the least in the Kingdom of heaven is greater than he."
   (Matt 11:11)

Reflection: Cassius Marcellus Clay Jr., later known as Muhammad Ali, won the Heavyweight Boxing Championship three times. He was not lacking pride. In his own words: "I am the greatest! . . . I'm the greatest thing that ever lived. I don't have a mark on my face, and I upset Sonny Liston, and I just turned twenty-two years old. I must be the greatest."

Jesus did not call John the Baptist the greatest person who ever lived, but Jesus did attribute greatness to the Baptist. He did so because John discerned God's will and he did it. We know the story: baptizing at the Jordan; calling people to repentance; confronting Herod in his sin; beheaded because of a woman's vengeance. Like Elijah, an earlier prophet, the Baptist fulfilled his mission in delivering God's message.

We are all called to be great; we are all called to holiness. And what does that holiness mean? According to Aelred

Squire in his work *Asking the Fathers*, "holiness consists in one thing only, namely, in faithfulness to God's plan—an active fidelity, in so far as we accomplish as best we can the duties in our state in life, a passive fidelity in so far as we accept and suffer with love whatever divine providence sends us."

Great! Greater! Greatest! In the end what matters is humility, living in the truth of things. If there is anything great in our lives, it is because of God's grace, a God who is the author of all that we have and are.

Meditation: In what sense can holiness be equated with greatness? Why is pride such a dangerous vice? How can we foster humility in this season of Advent?

Prayer: Loving God, you grasp us by the hand and lead us down the road of holiness. Herein lies our greatness: discerning and doing your will. May we emulate John the Baptist in having ears to hear your voice. May we emulate John's courage in doing what you ask.

December 12: Our Lady of Guadalupe (Catholic Church)
Friday of the Second Week of Advent (Episcopal Church)

Singing and Rejoicing

Readings: Zech 2:14-17 or Rev 11:19a; 12:1-6a, 10ab;
Luke 1:26-38 or Luke 1:39-47

Scripture:
Sing and rejoice, O daughter Zion!
See, I am coming to dwell among you, says the LORD.
   (Zech 2:14)

Reflection: Carl Jung (1875–1961), the Swiss psychologist,
had etched on his tombstone the words *Vocatus atque non
vocatus Deus aderit* ("Bidden or not bidden, God is present").
That same phrase was carved on the front door of his house.
Jung believed in the presence of God whether or not a person
is conscious of this faith fact.

On this feast of Our Lady of Guadalupe we ponder in
Luke's gospel the great mystery of the incarnation, God-
become-flesh in the womb of Mary. Though God was present
in all of creation, in all moments of time and space, now a
new and startling presence breaks into history. Mary said
"yes" to the invitation to become the mother of Jesus. She
was "bidden" and she accepted the call.

It was in 1531 when Juan Diego experienced the presence
of Mary in his life. In that appearance, Mary identified herself
as a compassionate and merciful mother, keenly aware of

the sorrows of the suffering. In response to this event the church now venerates Mary as the Patroness of the Americas and as the Protectress of the Unborn. Bidden or not, Mary intercedes for all people who are hurting, for all life that is in harm's way.

What the prophet Zechariah tells us, that God is coming to dwell among us, was fulfilled in a unique way in the annunciation story. Because of this coming, that divine presence, we have cause to sing and rejoice. Because Mary came to Juan Diego, gracing him with her compassionate presence, we have cause to sing and rejoice.

Though Carl Jung died many years ago, his influence still abides, especially for those who visit his gravesite or enter his house. "Bidden or not bidden, God is present." Let us sing and rejoice.

Meditation: What is your sense of the presence of God? How is it that if God is present everywhere, so many people do not register that presence on their radar screen?

Prayer: Compassionate and merciful Mary, Jesus came and dwelt in you. You received him with love and tenderness. Jesus comes to us, too, in the Eucharist. Help us to appreciate more and more his abiding love; help us to share Jesus' presence by living lives of compassion and mercy.

December 13: Saint Lucy, Virgin and Martyr
(Catholic Church)

Saturday of the Second Week of Advent (Episcopal Church)

Words: Prophetic and Transformative

Readings: Sir 48:1-4, 9-11; Matt 17:9a, 10-13

Scripture:
In those days,
like a fire there appeared the prophet Elijah
   whose words were as a flaming furnace. (Sir 48:1)

Reflection: Elijah! John the Baptist! Jesus! Lucy! In today's Advent feast, we witness the power of God's word, proclaimed and lived in the lives of prophets and saints. It is a word as strong as fire and a word that illumines the world. It is a word that burns but does not consume. Rather, it purifies and refines whatever it touches.

What are some of the names given to God's fiery words? The supreme one is love, because God is love. Love is the energy that creates unity and overflows into joy and peace. Love gave Elijah the power to be God's messenger; love gave John the Baptist the courage to proclaim the truth; love gave St. Lucy the grace to remain true to her calling. And, of course, Jesus is the manifestation of God's love, God's glory blazing on the mountain slopes and in every dark valley.

Another fiery word of God is wisdom. In Jesus, the disciples came to recognize the very presence of God. They were gifted with understanding and insight, their blindness lifted and their ignorance taken away. They recognized in Jesus the fulfillment of the law and the prophets. They recognized in Jesus their brother, friend, and redeemer.

Saint Francis de Sales, that master of metaphors, wrote, "Doctors derive much knowledge of the health or sickness of a man by looking at his tongue; and our words are true indications of the qualities of our souls" (*Introduction to the Devout Life*). As we hear down the ages the words of Elijah and Jesus, the Baptist and St. Lucy, we know not only the quality of their souls but also the meaning of life. Let us listen carefully.

Meditation: What significance do you assign to the written and spoken word? What biblical words or passages have been like fire to you?

Prayer: Saint Lucy, patroness of the blind, help us to see and hear the will of God. So often we are blind to God's presence; too often we are deaf to God's word. We stand in need of God's grace. Intercede for us in this Advent season so that our hearts and minds might be well prepared to celebrate the Christmas mysteries.

THIRD WEEK OF ADVENT

God's Will

Readings: Isa 61:1-2a, 10-11; 1 Thess 5:16-24; John 1:6-8, 19-28

Scripture:
Rejoice always. Prayer without ceasing.
In all circumstances give thanks,
    for this is the will of God for you in Christ Jesus.
        (1 Thess 5:16)

Reflection: The question of God's will haunts the human spirit. What exactly is it that God is asking us to do or to be? Micah the prophet is helpful here: "Only to do justice and to love goodness, / and to walk humbly with your God" (Mic 6:8). So too the Scripture scholar Walter Brueggemann when he writes, "And we know from Jesus and from our whole history that he wills freedom, at-homeness and life. He has sworn his unending hostility to slavery, exile and death." Saint Paul is also clear in saying that God's will is that we rejoice at all times, pray night and day, and give God our thanks.

"Rejoice always." One might wonder if St. Paul knew what he was talking about since all of human history is filled with cruelty, violence, and death. Yet it was Paul who knew personally the experience of suffering. He was beaten, shipwrecked, rejected by his own, and martyred. Yet here he is saying "Rejoice always."

Paul grounded this imperative in a deep conviction that God's love embraced him and the world. It is the awareness of this grace that leads to joy and rejoicing. Despite the "slings and arrows" of life, God's abiding presence makes possible a joy-filled disposition.

"[N]ever cease praying." Prayer is communion and communication with God. In this dialogue we experience a "mutual presence" and share our common joys and sorrows. Although formal prayer may be sporadic, there is another type of prayer that continues night and day. It is a frame of mind by which we refer all our thoughts and actions to the indwelling presence of God.

"[R]ender constant thanks." Gratitude must characterize the Christian life. All is gift; all is grace. Thanksgiving becomes a way of life and that thanksgiving is expressed in generosity. We give thanks for the great mysteries of our faith: creation, redemption, sanctification. We give thanks for the sea and stars and mountains; we give thanks for the Bethlehem mystery and the Calvary drama; we give thanks for the fire and wind of Pentecost, the gift of the Holy Spirit.

Saint Paul is an excellent Advent mentor and model.

Meditation: What are the imperatives that govern your life? What roles do rejoicing, praying, and giving thanks have in your life?

Prayer: Saint Paul, intercede for us. Pray that we might know the cause for joy; that we might pray to God in all the seasons of our life; that we might be a eucharistic people, giving thanks for all that comes our way. May we have the faith and courage that sustained your life and may we come, one day, to experience the victory of the cross.

December 15: Monday of the Third Week of Advent

A Delicate Balance

Readings: Num 24:2-7, 15-17a; Matt 21:23-27

Scripture:
"By what authority are you doing these things?
And who gave you this authority?" (Matt 21:23b)

Reflection: In John W. O'Malley's *What Happened at Vatican II*, we are given an excellent overview of the role of authority in the Christian life. O'Malley talks about the teaching authority of the church (the magisterium) and how that authority relates to the authority of Scripture and tradition. As followers of Jesus we are aware of the power of God's word (Scripture), the richness of our two thousand years of history (tradition), and the importance of our teachers in the faith (magisterium). All three of these authorities have much to tell us and they need to be held in a delicate balance.

During this Advent season we turn to *the* authority in our Christian life: Jesus! He is the one who heals, preaches, and teaches with authority. Time and time again we are told that this authority was given to him by the Father. There is no ambiguity here; there is no need to question further. And yet the elders and the people found it difficult to believe that someone so apparently like themselves could act and teach in this supreme manner.

As we continue our journey of faith, we exercise our freedom in the context of authority. John Henry Cardinal

Newman (1801–90), considered by some to be the father of Vatican II, speaks powerfully of the concept of authority and the need for balance in his *Apologia Pro Vita Sua*: "Conscience is an authority; the Bible is an authority; such is the Church; such is Antiquity; such are the words of the wise; such are hereditary lessons; such are ethical truths; such are historical memories, such are legal saws and state maxims; such are proverbs, such are sentiments, presages, and prepossessions." It is no wonder the elders questioned Jesus about authority given the fact that there are so many sources for it.

Meditation: What/who are the authorities in your life? In what way do you exercise authority? Do you find that your conscience is a reliable authority?

Prayer: Lord Jesus, may we be submissive to your divine authority. Grant us the courage to use our freedom in a healthy way, doing not what we want to do, but doing what we ought to do. Heal our rebellious hearts; redeem our nomadic souls. Come, Lord Jesus, come.

December 16: Tuesday of the Third Week of Advent

A Change of Mind

Readings: Zeph 3:1-2, 9-13; Matt 21:28-32

Scripture:
" 'Son, go out and work in the vineyard today.'
The son said in reply, 'I will not,'
   but afterwards he changed his mind and went."
     (Matt 21:28b-29)

Reflection: John the Baptist preached a gospel of repentance for the forgiveness of sin. Interestingly, such people as tax collectors and prostitutes, considered by many as public sinners, listened to him and had a change of mind and of heart and, yes, a change of lifestyle. By contrast, the chief priests and elders, those who were considered righteous and learned, found John's message either unnecessary or wrong. For whatever reason, they did not "change their minds" and went on their merry way outside of the company of Jesus, God's very presence of mercy and love.

Change is difficult at many levels: intellectual, emotional, moral. We become set in our ways and defy preachers and teachers, saints and prophets who try to convert us into new ways of thinking or feeling or acting. We too can go on our merry way, missing out on truth and goodness and beauty.

Cardinal Newman captured well the importance of change in his famous maxim: "In a higher world it is otherwise, but here below to live is to change, and to be perfect is to have changed often." Whether we like it or not, we are always in a state of transition and the choice is one of growth or diminishment, a choice of obedience or disobedience, to the nudges, whispers, proddings of an ever-present God. The two sons in the gospel parable exemplify one of the fundamental options in life: the doing or not doing of God's will.

Meditation: What is the history of "change" in your life? Do you agree with Cardinal Newman's contention that "to live is to change"?

Prayer: Come, Holy Spirit. Grace us with the gift of obedience and a willingness to change. Our minds are often opinionated; our hearts are often numb; our behavior indifferent. Enlighten us to truly see your plan; enkindle our hearts with the Pentecostal fire; empower us to do what is right and just.

Genealogy: Jesus' Family Tree

Readings: Gen 49:2, 8-10; Matt 1:1-17

Scripture:
The book of the genealogy of Jesus Christ,
    the son of David, the son of Abraham. (Matt 1:1)

Reflection: To know someone, indeed, to know ourselves, a genealogy can be most helpful. By studying our family history and tracing our lineage, we are given a perspective that can be truly enlightening (and scary). Be the source of knowledge from oral tradition, historical records, or medical charts, we realize to some degree why we think, feel, and act the way we do.

Jesus was born into the human family. Our God came to live among us and embraced the human condition. Jesus experienced our poverty of spirit, our limitations of time and space, the anxieties of the human heart. Indeed, we have a "scandal of particularity"—that Jesus came here at a particular time and in a particular place to a particular people and culture. Such is the love of our God for us.

But look carefully at his family history: David! True, he was a handsome, ruddy youth. True, he was a courageous leader and king. But also true, he committed murder and adultery. Jesus, the son of David, knew of the dark side of this ancestor.

Again, look carefully at Jesus' family history: Abraham. What a man of faith! When God called, Abraham left his homeland and did what the Lord commanded him. What nobility and courage and outright obedience. But look again: Abraham who was not above lying and deception and a harshness that is startling. Jesus, the son of Abraham, knew of the weakness of our human nature in his ancestor Abraham.

Murray Bowen (1913–90), a psychiatrist who taught at Georgetown University, developed a theory of family therapy based on the idea that our emotional experiences can be understood in the context of the extended family unit. If accurate, then the emotional life of Jesus, Mary, and Joseph must be seen and appreciated in the light of their genealogies. To have David and Abraham at the kitchen table helps us to understand the beauty and complexity of our human existence.

Meditation: How well do you know your family genealogy? Does your genealogy include the person of Jesus (and his relatives)? In what ways does our family history shape our thinking, feeling, and acting?

Prayer: Jesus, son of David and son of Abraham, help us to appreciate the trials and tribulations of the human journey. Like David and Abraham, we too struggle with temptations of the flesh and soul. Like them, we need your mercy and forgiveness. Grant us the grace of insight and conversion during this Advent season.

December 18: Thursday in Late Advent

"O Adonai"

Readings: Jer 23:5-8; Matt 1:18-25

Scripture:
Behold, the days are coming, says the LORD,
   when I will raise up a righteous shoot to David.
      (Jer 23:5a)

Reflection: As we approach the Christmas mystery the rich liturgical tradition of the Church provides us with the "O" antiphons, traditionally sung at Vespers during the last seven days before Christmas. They impart a heightened sense of yearning, one that is even further intensified when followed by the *Magnificat*, Mary's song of praise (as is the case in *The Liturgy of the Hours*). The antiphon traditionally sung on December 18 celebrates the fact that the God who gave Moses the law on Sinai has now come to live among us in Jesus, to rescue us from sin and death. What mighty power we have here.

Known as "O Adonai," this antiphon reads,

O Adonái et Dux domus Israel, qui Móysi in igne flammæ rubi apparuisti, et ei in Sina legem dedisti: veni ad rediméndum nos in brácchio exténto.

O Adonai and Ruler of the house of Israel, you appeared to Moses in the flame of the burning bush, and on Mount Sinai gave him your law. Come, and with an outstretched arm redeem us.

It is in Jesus, Emmanuel, that our redemption is won, that restoration to unity is achieved. In verse form we might ponder this great antiphon:

> A Lord we have familiar with bushes,
> burning ones at that, unconsumed.
> A Lord we have dwelling on a mountain,
> offering paths on how to achieve the peak.
> A Redeemer we have, embracing a lonely people,
> bringing us home, hand in hand.

Meditation: What does this antiphon say to you? How has the law of Moses (the Ten Commandments) and the law of Jesus impacted your spiritual journey?

Prayer: Providential and loving God, you who are present in fire and law, guiding us still, come and take us by the hand. Then, and only then, shall we be saved. May we see you in every bush and bird, may we obey your slightest whisper and glance. Lead us home; make us whole. Come, Jesus—O Adonai, come. Maranatha. Veni, Jesu—O Adonai, veni.

December 19: Friday in Late Advent

Samson and John the Baptist

Readings: Judg 13:2-7, 24-25a; Luke 1:5-25

Scripture:
The woman bore a son and named him Samson.
The boy grew up and the LORD blessed him;
  the Spirit of the LORD stirred him. (Judg 13:24-25a)

Reflection: Two barren women, Manoah's wife and Elizabeth, Zechariah's wife, each bore a son. Two angels were on duty bearing good news. One came to Manoah's wife and the other to Zechariah. Two instructions were given regarding food and drink. The boys born were to be teetotalers. Two missions were assigned the sons, to carry God's Spirit into the world.

Samson, a judge and warrior of the ancient Israelites, was a person of great strength and considerable ire. He dispatched a lion and a good portion of an army (using a jaw bone of an ass), he laid ruin to a pagan temple, and he got in trouble for his relationship with Delilah, who betrayed him. After being blinded by his enemies, Samson died in the temple of the Dagon as he pushed the pillars aside, bringing down the building upon him and the Philistines.

John the Baptist, a cousin of Jesus and a reformer, was a person of great integrity and courage. We know the story: his confrontation with Herod for living with his brother's wife, the wrath of Herodias, and John's beheading. But John completed what God had begun in him by preaching a baptism of repentance. Many came to the Jordan River and were baptized for the forgiveness of sin. John's death, so different from Samson's demise, makes manifest how human decisions lead to consequences of great significance.

In the stories of the conception and birth of Samson and John, we see the foreshadowing of Jesus' coming into the world. Again an angel is sent, new life is promised, and the Spirit of God is astir in human history. The stories of all three—Samson, John, and Jesus—end in violence but not before their missions are accomplished.

Meditation: Are angels still being sent in our postmodern age? Who are the messengers sent from God bearing the promise of new life?

Prayer: God of wisdom and strength, help us to discern our mission in life and give us the courage to collaborate in your plan of redemption. May we not abuse our power; may we not shrink from doing your will, whatever the cost. Through your Spirit of fortitude and knowledge we will do as you command and know the peace that is beyond all understanding.

December 20: Saturday in Late Advent

Telltale Signs: Large and Small

Readings: Isa 7:10-14; Luke 1:26-38

Scripture:
The LORD spoke to Ahaz:
Ask for a sign from the LORD, your God;
   let it be deep as the nether world, or high as the sky!
      (Isa 7:10-11)

Reflection: Signs can tell a small tale, as when the car ahead of us has a flashing light indicating the car will be making a right turn. Signs can also tell a large tale, as when the Lord informed the wearisome Ahaz that a virgin will conceive and bear a son. Of course, this large telltale sign is repeated in the gospel, as Mary is the one who, though not married, will conceive and bear the child Jesus.

Signs have the ability to translate inner thoughts and feelings into outer expression. A young man gives to his girlfriend a ring to symbolize his love, affection, and commitment. A mother sits by her sick child the whole night through and we know in that deed the utter concern of a mother's love. Or, by contrast, the absence of a parent to his or her family reveals irresponsibility and a want of commitment. Our words and deeds, signs large and small, speak volumes.

Our God, Emmanuel, comes to us, as he came to Ahaz and Mary, in signs and deeds. We call these moments our sacramental life. Through the water of baptism, through the oil used in confirmation, anointing, and holy orders, through the words of marriage, through the bread and wine of the Eucharist, through the absolution formula, God is made present and manifest. These are large telltale signs of God's love. But God also comes in small telltale signs such as words of affirmation and confrontation, such as moments of successes and failures, such as a bird's song and a sunset.

Louis-Marie Chauvet, a professor of sacramental theology, writes in *The Sacraments*, "Like our body, our mind needs two legs to walk straight: sign and symbol." Ahaz was given a sign as was Mary. They walked straight in doing God's will.

Meditation: What signs have you been given to assure you of God's presence and love? What signs have you given to others to assure them of your concern and affection?

Prayer: God of sign and symbol, may we discern your abiding presence in the ordinary events of our life. Your promise of presence assures us that you are with us here and now. Deepen our faith to apprehend your nearness and aid us in responding by living a life of discipleship. Come, Lord Jesus, come.

FOURTH WEEK OF ADVENT

Advent Solitude

Readings: 2 Sam 7:1-5, 8b-12, 14a, 16; Rom 16:25-27; Luke 1:26-38

Scripture:
The angel Gabriel was sent from God
   to a town of Galilee called Nazareth,
   to a virgin betrothed to a man named Joseph . . .
Then the angel departed from her. (Luke 1:26-27a, 38b)

Reflection: Comings and goings! Approaches and departures! Being sent and returning. And in between the drama of life unfolds. The angel Gabriel came to Mary and we hear her emotional response. Mary was afraid and was puzzled by the message. After graced assurance, the angel departed. Now alone, we might wonder, what happened in the heart of Mary?

We know a part of the rest of the story. Mary hastened to her cousin Elizabeth and the two women shared how God was working so mysteriously in their lives. Once again we get a glimpse of the social nature of our lives, how desperately we need one another to unravel and deal with the mysteries that surround us. Traveling and living alone has its dangers. Eventually, we realize that we are in life's joys and sorrows together and our self-reliance is essentially fictional. Like the community of the Trinity, we are at the bottom communal in nature.

Yet, this being said, we also need our solitude, time apart to reflect on and process the many experiences of our life. When the angel Gabriel departed from Mary, she pondered anew what God's plan was for her. Out of that solitude arose one of the great canticles of all time as Mary would proclaim to Elizabeth and to the world, "My soul proclaims the greatness of the Lord / . . . the Almighty has done great things for me."

In her reflective work *Gift from the Sea*, Anne Morrow Lindbergh writes, "Certain springs are tapped only when we are alone. The artist knows he must be alone to create; the writer, to work out his thoughts; the musician, to compose; the saint, to pray." Mary experienced that aloneness to our great benefit.

Meditation: How do you balance the individual and social dimensions of your life? What role does solitude play in your spiritual journey?

Prayer: Mary, be with us on our Advent journey. As you said yes to what God asked of you, may we follow your example. Pray for our family and friends as we gather together; pray for the moments of solitude and silence that nurture our union with your son, Jesus. May we too realize the great things that God has done for us.

December 22: Monday in Late Advent

Hannah and Mary: Agents of Glory

Readings: 1 Sam 1:24-28; Luke 1:46-56

Scripture:
She [Hannah] left Samuel there. (1 Sam 1:28b)

Mary remained with Elizabeth about three months
   and then returned to her home. (Luke 1:56)

Reflection: Hannah, Mary, and Elizabeth! Samuel, Jesus, and John the Baptist. These Advent days are filled with pregnant women, babies destined to greatness, canticles that reach to the heavens. Perhaps we have here something that looks like glory, the glory of God breaking into history in humble, powerful, startling ways.

Hannah was a woman of prayer. Her desire was to bear a child and her wish was granted. Then she and her husband came to the temple with their offerings, not only of flour, wine, and a bull, but also the presentation of their child Samuel. What God gave Hannah was then dedicated back to the Lord. What a life of faith, this deep awareness that God is the origin of all that we have and are, a faith that returns to the Lord what is his.

Mary was a woman of prayer and her prayer of praise rings down through the centuries in her *Magnificat*. The great thing done for her was similar to that of Hannah, the gift of a son. And, like Hannah, Mary would come to the temple for her presentation. Mary would offer back to God the most precious possession she had: her son Jesus! We have on this Advent day examples of two women who knew and practiced the art of living and the art of dying.

Hannah and Mary were instruments of glory, that fullness of being and light and love. We see glimpses of glory in a double rainbow, in a golden wheat field, in an act of kindness. But full glory comes in moments of total self-giving, a self-giving that emulates the very mystery of God. Glorious is Hannah's offering of her son; glorious is Mary's canticle that sings the truth of God's grace; and glorious is the mystery of the cross that is already foreshadowed by two mothers who knew how to give back to God their greatest treasure.

Meditation: Where have you seen God's glory manifest in this Advent season? In what ways have you been an agent of God's glory, of God's light, love, and life? What is your greatest treasure?

Prayer: Self-giving God, help us to emulate the example of Hannah and Mary in their act of total self-donation. May we realize that we are but stewards of all your gifts, caretakers of our relationships and possessions. When you ask for what we have or are, may we will to sacrifice everything. Only with your grace can we truly become Advent people.

December 23: Tuesday in Late Advent

Waiting Ended

Readings: Mal 3:1-4, 23-24; Luke 1:57-66

Scripture:
When the time arrived for Elizabeth to have her child
   she gave birth to a son. (Luke 1:57)

Reflection: The waiting was over for Elizabeth. She gave birth to her son and he was named John. We know the rest of the story. Salvation history had reached its high point with the arrival of Elizabeth's son John, and Mary's son Jesus.

Our Advent waiting is coming to an end. In two days we will celebrate the Nativity of the Lord. Like Elizabeth, Mary too had the experience of looking forward to the day of delivery. And we, the church, look forward to the Christmas coming of our Lord and the gift of our salvation. Waiting is a major part of our human journey as it is of our Christian existence. But, in faith, we do wait in joyful hope.

John Henry Cardinal Newman, in his *Apologia Pro Vita Sua*, wrote about being made ill by suspense: "[I] felt the weariness of waiting, and the sickness of delayed hope." Indeed, waiting can make us weary and hope deferred can cause sickness. Waiting for the lab report, waiting for news of a lost son or daughter, waiting for consolation after a tragic loss can be overwhelming. But now the Lord is here and the church and the world rejoice. A child is born, the Savior of the world!

All this is, of course, a matter of faith. In our contemporary culture the Christian narrative is not the predominant story. Christians are a cognitive minority; our story is not held by most people. Yet, for that, we do put all our hope in one basket, the person of Jesus born of Mary. And it was the prophet, John the Baptist, who prepared the way by preaching the forgiveness of sin.

Let the rejoicing begin. Let our alleluias ring out.

Meditation: What has been your experience of waiting? Have weariness and sickness been part of that experience?

Prayer: Gracious God, come to our aid. We find it difficult to wait; we grow impatient with grace delayed. Fill us with joyful hope, knowing that you give us what we need, and guide us on this perilous journey. And when you come, may our minds and hearts be open to receive your Son.

December 24: Wednesday in Late Advent (Christmas Eve)

Holiness/Righteousness

Readings: 2 Sam 7:1-5, 8b-12, 14a, 16; Luke 1:67-79

Scripture:
"This was the oath he swore to our father Abraham:
   to set us free from the hand of our enemies,
   free to worship him without fear,
   holy and righteous in his sight
      all the days of our life." (Luke 1:73-75)

Reflection: God's promise of freedom is at the heart of the Christmas mystery. Jesus is the one sent to free us from our slavery to sin and our fear of mortality. As the "O" antiphons remind us during this octave of Christmas, our salvation is near at hand.

Our response involves two things: our striving for holiness and our living lives of righteousness. Interiorly, we are called to live in the presence of the Lord; externally, we are called to do what is right and just. Holiness and righteousness are two ways in which we worship and give praise to our God.

So what is holiness? The Quaker Douglas Steere responds in this way: "The life of sanctity is a mad response to the initiative of the mad love of God that has come into a realization that God holds it in the utter consuming, transforming, energizing irradiation of His costly love" (*Together in Solitude*). Holiness is the perfection of love; holiness is being connected to God as the branch is connected to the vine. This connection leads to fruitfulness and makes us agents of the kingdom.

So what is righteousness? It has something to do with integrity and justice, with a moral life that follows God's divine plan. Saint Paul teaches that righteousness is more God's work through the death and resurrection of Jesus, but it also involves our cooperation. The New Testament reminds us that faith without loving deeds is dead. Salvation comes through the grace of the paschal mystery; righteousness—being right with God—also demands serious moral striving to do good.

Saints are holy and righteous. In *The Varieties of Religious Experience* William James gives us a beautiful description of sanctity: "The saints, with their extravagance of human tenderness, are the great torch-bearers of this belief [the essential sacredness of everyone], the tip of the wedge, the clearers of the darkness."

Meditation: Is there a difference between being holy and righteous? Who are the people in your life who clear the darkness and give light to others?

Prayer: Saving God, give us the grace to be light and love to others. It is you who make us holy and righteous. It is you who empower us to love and do good. In the gift of Jesus we see manifest the one who scatters darkness for all of us who dwell under the shadow of death. Come, Lord Jesus, come.

SEASON OF CHRISTMAS

December 25: The Nativity of the Lord (Christmas)

God's Promise Fulfilled

Readings:
VIGIL: Isa 62:1-5; Acts 13:16-17, 22-25; Matt 1:1-25
    (or 1:18-25)
MIDNIGHT: Isa 9:1-6; Titus 2:11-14; Luke 2:1-14
DAWN: Isa 62:11-12; Titus 3:4-7; Luke 2:15-20
DAY: Isa 52:7-10; Heb 1:1-6; John 1:1-18 (or 1:1-5, 9-14)

Scripture:
And the Word became flesh
    and made his dwelling among us,
    and we saw his glory,
    the glory as of the Father's only Son,
    full of grace and truth. (John 1:14)

Reflection: The mysteries of our faith cannot be adequately captured in words. Language is unable to do full justice to reality. So we turn to metaphorical language and to poetry in our attempt to fathom the Nativity of the Lord. Here is one vain attempt of mine:

Christmas Day

One poet said that you "tumbled" down to earth
    whereas the church says you leaped down.
Either way you came
    and we are overwhelmed by the nearness of our God.

Is it possible for Eternity to be imprisoned by Time?
Is it possible for Divinity to assume our lowly Humanity?
Our minds reel at the mystery of the Incarnation
whereas our hearts throb with joy and wonder.

Another Christmas Day,
another gathering of the church
to celebrate the Word made flesh.
How is it possible not to sing,
in the silent watches of the night,
our "Joy to the World," our "Come, let us adore him"?

It is in Jesus that the fullness of grace and truth is made present and manifest. It is in Jesus, the Word made flesh, that we have that blessed assurance of God's abiding love. On this Christmas Day we pay homage to a God whose love is extravagant and whose mercy is without end. Joy to the world, indeed. And, yes, peace to people of goodwill.

Meditation: Who are the poets who help you delve into the mysteries of our faith? George Herbert in his poem "Trinity Sunday"? Edgar Allan Poe in his poem "Hymn"? Jessica Powers in her poem "The Master Beggar"?

Prayer: Jesus, we see you in the crib and on the cross, and come to know something of the mystery of your love. In taking on our flesh you know from the inside our birthing and our dying, our joys and our sorrows. On this Christmas Day help us to praise and glorify you for all you have done for us.

The Two Hands of God

Readings: Acts 6:8-10; 7:54-59; Matt 10:17-22

Scripture:
But he [Stephen], filled with the Holy Spirit,
   looked up intently to heaven
     and saw the glory of God and Jesus standing at the right
     hand of God. (Acts 7:55)

Reflection: One of the most important theologians at the Second Vatican Council was the Dominican priest Yves Congar. His sense of ecumenism and the working of the Holy Spirit were themes that influenced many of the sixteen documents. In his book *I Believe in the Holy Spirit* Congar wrote, "Irenaeus expressed the derivation of the Church from the two missions, that of the Word and that of the Breath, in a poetical manner in the image of the two hands of God."

That poetic language is also found in today's reading from Acts. Stephen, the church's first martyr, saw God's glory and "Jesus standing at the right hand of God." Here is the Word, the eternal Son of God. And at God's left hand, the Breath, the Holy Spirit. Again, Congar wrote, "The Church, as an organism of knowledge and love, is entirely dependent on these missions [of Word and Spirit]."

Stephen was involved in both missions of the church. He was an agent of knowledge, filled with God's power and grace. In debating with the people of his day, he proclaimed Jesus as the Son of Man. This proclamation incensed the crowds and Stephen was stoned to death.

More, Stephen was an agent of love, being an instrument of the Holy Spirit. Even as he was being killed Stephen prayed that God would have mercy on his persecutors. What love we witness here, what power of the Holy Spirit.

Knowledge and love! Jesus and the Holy Spirit! The two hands of God guiding the church in its central mission. And Stephen has become for all Christians a mentor and a model of discipleship.

Meditation: What is your understanding of the mission of the church? Does the image of the hand of God speak to you? In what ways are you an agent of God's knowledge and love?

Prayer: Saint Stephen, pray for us. May our sins, be they big or small, not be held against us. Pray that we might have your courage and wisdom, your compassion and love. May we, like you, look up to heaven and come to know the knowledge of Christ and the love of the Holy Spirit, the Word and Breath of God.

December 27: Saint John, Apostle and Evangelist

John the Evangelist: A Short Bio

Readings: 1 John 1:1-4; John 20:1a, 2-8

Scripture:
On the first day of the week,
  Mary Magdalene ran and went to Simon Peter
  and to the other disciple whom Jesus loved, and told them,
  "They have taken the Lord from the tomb,
  and we do not know where they put him." (John 20:1a-2)

Reflection: We know a few things about John the Evangelist. He was the son of Zebedee and the brother of James; he was an apostle of Jesus and loved by the Lord; he was a believer and an evangelist. Also, he was able to outrun Peter on their way to the empty tomb.

But there is more. John wrote down his experience of faith. What he heard and what he had seen regarding Jesus, the Word of life, he had to share. Part of the motive for this was that John's joy was not complete until others were also aware that eternal life is in store for us. As Emily Dickinson says, "This World is not conclusion." John the Evangelist was a writer, telling the world that *this* world lacks finality. In Jesus, we are destined for eternal life.

There is yet another chapter in the life of John the apostle. Fast-forward to the scene of Calvary. As Jesus was about to die, he entrusted his mother to John's care. We don't know exactly what that entailed, but we do know that in his gesture Jesus showed the greatest respect for the beloved disciple.

During this Christmas season we continue to see the great things that God has done and is doing for the world: the courage of Stephen in proclaiming the good news; the evangelizing work of John the Evangelist; the feast of the Holy Family. How rich is our liturgy and our tradition. How blessed we are to be a part of salvation history.

Meditation: What passages in John's gospel speak most deeply to you? In what ways have you shared your faith with others? In words? In deeds? By a Christian lifestyle?

Prayer: Gracious and loving God, help us feel the urgency of our call to be evangelists. May we, like Mary Magdalene, Peter, and John, learn how to *run* in search of you. May we be willing to share with others what we have seen and heard regarding the mysteries of our faith.

December 28: The Holy Family of Jesus, Mary, and Joseph
(Catholic Church)

Fourth Day in the Octave of Christmas (Episcopal Church)

Family: The Domestic Church

Readings: Sir 3:2-6, 12-14 or Gen 15:1-6; 21:1-3; Col 3:12-21 or
3:12-17 or Heb 11:8, 11-12, 17-19; Luke 2:22-40 or 2:22, 39-40

Scripture:
God sets a father in honor over his children;
    a mother's authority he confirms over her sons. (Sir 3:2)

Reflection: Over the years our liturgical books undergo revision. In the process, some favorite texts are no longer available and a sense of loss can be felt. In our previous Sacramentary, there was an alternative prayer for the feast of the Holy Family that was powerful in its content and style. It is worthy of both our contemplation and our memorizing:

Father in heaven, creator of all,
you ordered the earth to bring forth life
and crowned its goodness by creating the family of man.
In history's moment when all was ready,
you sent your Son to dwell in time,
obedient to the laws of life in our world.
Teach us the sanctity of human love,
show us the value of family life,
and help us to live in peace with all men
that we may share in your life for ever.

"Teach us the sanctity of human love"! We are all lifelong learners and we do well to ask God's Spirit to instruct us time and time again about the holiness of human love. This love will involve respect, reverence, and responsibility toward others and ourselves.

"[S]how us the value of family life"! We are social by nature and desperately need one another. There are few blessings greater than being reared in a good family. In a culture of radical individualism we need the grace to regain a sense of the common good.

"[H]elp us to live in peace with all [people]"! Jesus' farewell gift to us is peace. God's plan is that we live in harmony with one another, with him, with all creation. And when peace comes, right behind will be its cousin joy.

Here is a prayer that deserves a place in our hearts.

Meditation: What has God taught you about human love? In what ways have you been an agent of peace in this Christmas season? What has been your experience of family life?

Prayer: Wise and loving God, instruct us in the matters of love. Deepen our bonds with family members and give us the courage to be instruments of your peace. Send your Spirit of prayer and action into our world. Veni, Creator Spiritus.

Orthodoxy/Orthopraxis

Readings: 1 John 2:3-11; Luke 2:22-35

Scripture:
Beloved:
The way we may be sure that we know Jesus
  is to keep his commandments.
Whoever says, "I know him," but does not keep his commandments
  is a liar, and the truth is not in him. (1 John 2:3-4)

Reflection: The question of knowing Jesus is fundamental
to Christian discipleship. We cannot love what we do not
know, but the opposite is also true: we cannot truly know if
we do not love. This paradox is not easy to unravel but John's
epistle is most helpful. Without qualification, John tells us
that we know Jesus by doing what he commands. We know
Jesus by following his way of forgiveness, compassion, and
love.

Orthodoxy, right thinking, is extremely important. The
playwright/philosopher Walter Kerr reminds us that an
infection begun in the mind will negatively affect one's entire
self. But orthodoxy has a first cousin: orthopraxis, right
doing. By emulating Jesus' lifestyle we know him by way of
participation.

When Jesus was brought to the temple for purification, Simeon was there and immediately "knew" who the child was. How so? Simeon was a righteous and devout man, guided by the Holy Spirit. It was not theology or some studied Christology that gave Simeon knowledge of Jesus, but rather a manner of living in the truth of things. So deep was the grace of this knowledge that Simeon predicted the future of this child and what Mary would have to suffer.

Like Simeon, Thomas Becket (1118–70), today's saint, came to embrace his office as the archbishop of Canterbury not by formal study (orthodoxy) but by the graces received from fasting and prayer (orthopraxis). Becket lived his discipleship by keeping God's commandments. Our challenge is to do the same.

Meditation: What is your understanding of the terms orthodoxy and orthopraxis? In what ways have you come to "know" Jesus over the years? Why are both study and practice important in the following of Jesus?

Prayer: Christ Jesus, may we come to know you in the breaking of the bread and in the sharing of the bread with others. May our obedience transform our minds and hearts into knowing and loving you more deeply. Guide us in your ways and we will know that peace that is far, far beyond all understanding.

December 30: Sixth Day in the Octave of Christmas

Towns: Ours and Yours

Readings: 1 John 2:12-17; Luke 2:36-40

Scripture:
When they [Joseph and Mary] had fulfilled all the prescrip-
    tions
    of the law of the Lord,
    they returned to Galilee,
    to their own town of Nazareth.
The child grew and became strong, filled with wisdom;
    and the favor of God was upon him. (Luke 2:39-40)

Reflection: Thornton Wilder's play *Our Town* was first performed in 1938. Many of us could identify with the presentation of what family life was like in our hometown.

Today we hear about Mary and Joseph returning to their
"own town of Nazareth." It was here that they would rear
their child Jesus who would grow to become strong and
wise, where the grace of God would be upon him. We are
not told of the neighbors next door, nor the evening gather-
ings or games, nor of tragedies or celebrations that transpired
in the town of Nazareth. But the ordinary events of a small
community are universal as we witness in Wilder's play.

Our growth as individuals is so dependent upon our environment and the people who populate it. Jesus had the
mentoring and modeling of Joseph and Mary. Jesus had the

richness of the Jewish tradition and its prayers and songs. Jesus experienced the importance of community and the power of customs.

One of the famous lines from *Our Town* is "Do any human beings ever realize life while they live it?" According to Pope Benedict XVI, Jesus taught us the art of living and the art of dying. Jesus was one who lived life to the full, the all of it. In whatever town we live, in whatever country we reside, let us realize and appreciate the life God has given to us.

Meditation: What memories do you have of growing up? Who were the people who taught you how to live and how to die? In your years of growing up, what or who was the major influence?

Prayer: Loving God, as we continue our Christmas journey may we continue to grow in our likeness to Christ. And, like him, may we find favor with you by living as he did, with obedience and self-giving. Instruct us daily in the art of living and dying. We make our prayer in Jesus' name.

The Divine Splendor

Readings: 1 John 2:18-21; John 1:1-18

Scripture:
No one has ever seen God.
The only-begotten Son, God, who is at the Father's side,
    has revealed him. (John 1:18)

Reflection: In the great musical *Les Misérables*, there is a powerful scene where three of the characters, Valjean, Fantine, and Éponine, sing of being led to salvation through the mystery of love. They proclaim together the truth that we see the face of God when we love another person.

The face of God has appeared in the person of Jesus, the Word made flesh. God is both present and manifest through the mystery of the incarnation. And Jesus is clear in stating that what we do to the least of our brothers and sisters we do to him. Thus, we continue to see God in those who enter our lives, be they ill or healthy, rich or poor, intelligent or wanting in education. God's ongoing revelation never ceases.

Again in today's gospel we read, "and we saw his glory, / the glory as of the Father's only-begotten Son, / full of grace and truth" (John 1:14b). Glory has something to do with life being lived to the full, with beauty and truth breaking forth into life, with radiance and grandeur. The face of an infant is as glorious as the evening sunset; the flight of a hawk is as glorious as a simple act of kindness; the compassionate word at a wake service is as glorious as the blooming of a hibiscus plant. But God's full glory is revealed in the life, death, resurrection, and ascension of Jesus Christ.

In his book *The Joy of the Gospel*, Cardinal Carlo Maria Martini writes, "The glory of which Scripture speaks repeatedly is the splendor of God, the overflowing of his power, the richness, goodness, and tenderness of God who intervenes in history. This is glory: the divine splendor which intervenes in history and is made visible." And we as a church cry out, *Gloria in excelsis Deo.*

Meditation: What are some experiences of God's glory on your spiritual journey? In what ways can we be instruments of God's glory to others?

Prayer: Glorious God, make us agents of your light and love. May we live life to the full, sharing with others the gifts you have given us. Through the gift of your Holy Spirit, may we discern your splendor in the works of creation and in the mission of your son Jesus. Come, Holy Spirit, come.

January 1: Solemnity of Mary, the Mother of God
(Catholic Church)

Holy Name of Jesus (Episcopal Church)

Mary's Prayer

Readings: Num 6:22-27; Gal 4:4-7; Luke 2:16-21

Scripture:
All who heard it [angels' message] were amazed
  by what had been told them by the shepherds.
And Mary kept all these things,
  reflecting on them in her heart. (Luke 2:18-19)

Reflection: Jesus' disciples approached him one day and asked their master how they were to pray. The disciples were given the *Pater Noster*, the "Our Father." We have all become beneficiaries of this great oration.

But within our rich tradition, another prayer has been given to us, namely, the *Ave Maria*, the "Hail Mary." On this feast of Mary's motherhood, we do well to reflect upon this prayer, and pray it from the heart.

Ave Maria, gratia plena, Dominus tecum! Mary, the mother of Jesus, is full of grace, filled with God's light, love, and life. And, indeed, the Lord is with her and us.

Benedicta tu in mulieribus, et benedictus fructus ventris tui, Iesus! Blessed is Mary among all women and blessed too the fruit of her womb, our Lord Jesus.

Sancta Maria, Mater Dei! Mary is the holy one, the loving, obedient servant of God. Mary is also the Mother of God, for we believe that Jesus is the eternal Son of God, both human and divine.

[O]ra pro nobis peccatoribus! Just as we pray to Mary, we ask her to pray for us. All of us have sinned and stand in need of God's mercy and compassion.

[N]unc, et in hora mortis nostrae! We ask Mary to pray for us in the present moment of our lives, whatever the circumstances may be. Also, we ask her intercession in the last hour that we spend on earth, whatever the circumstances.

Just as the early disciples asked Jesus for assistance in their prayer life and were granted the Lord's Prayer, so we too who ask for similar help have been given Mary's prayer to nurture our relationship with God.

Meditation: What are your three favorite prayers? How did these orations come to you? Whom have you taught to pray?

Prayer: Mary, mother of Jesus and mother of the church, continue to pray for us who travel this earthly journey. We need protection and guidance; we need forgiveness and God's mercy. May we emulate your life of obedience and self-giving. We have confidence that our prayers will be heard and granted through you.

*January 2: Saints Basil the Great and Gregory Nazianzen,
Bishops and Doctors of the Church*

The Art of Incognito

Readings: 1 John 2:22-28; John 1:19-28

Scripture:
John answered them [Pharisees],
   "I baptize with water;
   but there is one among you whom you do not recognize,
   the one who is coming after me,
   whose sandal strap I am not worthy to untie."
   (John 1:26-27)

Reflection: John the Baptist recognized his cousin Jesus as
the Lamb of God, the one who came to take away our sins
and break the chains of death. John's mission was one of
preparation, paving the way for the true Messiah. At the
Jordan River John baptized with water and called the people
of his day to repentance.

Most people did not recognize Jesus in his true identity.
The same is true today. Jesus continues to be present to the
world in many ways: in the Scriptures, in the sacraments, in
the community. Saint Basil the Great (ca. 330–79), whose feast
we celebrate today, had a profound faith in Jesus. In his life
as a monk and bishop, Basil was deeply concerned about the
poor and issues of social justice. In erecting a hospital and
orphanage, this doctor and bishop of the church did the

works of both charity and mercy. Basil saw Jesus in the faces and needs of the poor.

Just as in his own day, so too in our times, Jesus often travels incognito. Divinity is disguised in the mantle of our human condition. Yet, Jesus' presence is ubiquitous if we have the eyes of faith. As to finding Christ in our times we might listen to this line from a letter of Flannery O'Connor, a great Southern Catholic writer: "You will have found Christ when you are concerned with other people's sufferings and not your own."

In her poem "The Master Beggar," the Carmelite Jessica Powers raises a provocative question to Jesus: "Must You take up Your post on every block / of every street?" And, of course, the answer is yes. Jesus, practicing the art of incognito, is on every street corner with his whispered "Please!"

Meditation: In what situations have you seen Jesus in the past week? Was it in your home, at school, in the office, on the street corner? Why has God decided to practice the art of incognito?

Prayer: Jesus, the hidden one, help us to discern your presence in our family members and in strangers, in the plight of the poor and the rich, in the crowded highways of our life. And once having recognized your presence, may we respond with charity and mercy. Grant us the grace of faith and wisdom in coming to know and love you.

Children of a Loving God

Readings: 1 John 2:29–3:6; John 1:29-34

Scripture:
See what love the Father has bestowed on us
    that we may be called the children of God.
Yet so we are. (1 John 3:1)

Reflection: Mark Medoff wrote a stage play, *Children of a Lesser God*, that was made into a dramatic film in 1986 starring William Hurt and Marlee Matlin. It was a story about the deaf community, at once moving and highly informative.

In the letter of St. John, we are told that we are children of God, not of a "lesser God," but of the God who sent his Son into the world. Such was the magnitude of God's love for us. We are not only children but also beloved sons and daughters of a loving Father. Hopefully, we are not deaf to this message.

Another John, known as the Baptist, encountered the Lamb of God, Jesus. The Baptist heard the good news that this Jesus was the Father's beloved as he emerged from the Jordan River: "And a voice came from heaven, 'You are my beloved Son; with you I am well pleased'" (Luke 3:22b). Although John's role was "lesser" than that of Jesus, indeed subordinated to his cousin, it was of tremendous significance. He prepared the way of the Lord and called people, through the baptism of water, to repentance.

Foundational to the Christian tenets is the dignity of every single human being. Made in the image and likeness of God, we have immortal worth. God is Father to us all, giving life to all creation. But it's more than life, it is also love. In being called children of God we can also hear in that calling the word "beloved," just as Jesus heard it at the Jordan. If so, there is no lesser God, and no lesser children.

Meditation: In what ways have you experienced the mystery of love in your life? What is your sense of the dignity and worth of every person?

Prayer: Loving God, too often we fail to realize the mystery of your love for us and for our brothers and sisters. Give us the grace to hear your call of being "beloved," and give us the grace to call others "beloved." In God's eyes, we are all "immortal diamonds," precious in his sight and treasured for all eternity.

EPIPHANY AND
BAPTISM OF THE LORD

January 4: The Epiphany of the Lord

The Feast of Seeing

Readings: Isa 60:1-6; Eph 3:2-3a, 5-6; Matt 2:1-12

Scripture:
Then you shall be radiant at what you see,
    your heart shall throb and overflow,
for the riches of the sea shall be emptied out before you,
    the wealth of nations shall be brought to you. (Isa 60:5)

Reflection: Of our five natural senses—seeing, hearing, smelling, tasting, touching—the ability to see often receives highest ranking. It is not that the other senses are any less significant, but most people would forego sight last of all.

The gift of seeing ranges far beyond just physical sight, important as that is. Seeing also involves "insight," seeing into things, with understanding and comprehension. "Now I see," says the student who just grasped the explanation of the Pythagorean theorem. The magi saw the star but they also saw in the infant Jesus something much more. Thus they gave gifts of gold, frankincense, and myrrh. Herod saw a threat to his power in the prophet's prediction about a ruler coming out of Bethlehem. And St. Paul saw in the person of Christ the promise of salvation for all peoples, even the Gentiles.

The New England poet Mary Oliver talks about the importance of walking slowly through life lest we miss the beauty that surrounds us. More, once we see, we are to "bow often." The magi did not hurry through life but saw the star, the child, the mother. And then, in great reverence, they bowed low as they presented their gifts. And we, two thousand years later, are still singing *Venite adoremus*.

C. S. Lewis, in *The Magician's Nephew*, a volume in *The Chronicles of Narnia*, offers this insight: "For what you see and hear depends a good deal on where you are standing; it also depends on what sort of person you are." The magi and Herod saw the same star, they looked for the same ruler, they responded so differently. Why? Because of who they were and where they were standing.

Meditation: What value do you assign to the gift of sight? How does our personality affect what we see and hear?

Prayer: God of wisdom, help us see. Too often we are blind to the workings of grace and deaf to your call. Free us from all slavery and addiction so that our vision might improve. Free us from self-preoccupation so that we might be for others in a life of service. Come, Lord Jesus, come.

January 5: Monday after Epiphany
Saint John Neumann, Bishop

Discernment: The Art of Arts

Readings: 1 John 3:22–4:6; Matt 4:12-17, 23-25

Scripture:
Beloved, do not trust every spirit
  but test the spirits to see whether they belong to God,
    because many false prophets have gone out into the
      world. (1 John 4:1)

Reflection: In all of our lives there are inner movements, urges, impulses, stirrings, whispers, proddings that we categorize as "spirits." Some people are more sensitive to this dimension of life than others, yet everyone has these inner movements. The challenge is to discern, to sort out those diverse spirits to see whether or not they lead to life or death, to love or hate, to light or darkness. Spiritual writers call this ability of sorting out the inner stirrings and impulses of our lives the art of discernment.

In yesterday's feast of Epiphany, the magi had to discern whether the warning in a dream was real or not. In today's gospel, Jesus heard about John's arrest and he discerned that now was the time to proclaim that the Father's kingdom was near. Saint John Neumann (1811–60), whose feast we celebrate today, felt the inner call to leave his home country of Bohemia and come to the United States in 1836. At work, in our homes, at school, the challenge is to be aware of and respond to those inner whispers of life.

In John's letter we hear about the spirit of truth and the spirit of deceit. The criterion indicating that we are in the realm of truth is if our lifestyle imitates that of Jesus, a lifestyle of love and compassion and forgiveness. By contrast, if we fail to love or forgive, we can be assured that our lives have yielded to the devil's deceit.

As the Latin American theologian Jon Sobrino reminds us, "The disciple living today . . . does possess one ultimate criterion for correct discernment, i.e., Jesus himself" (*Christology at the Crossroads*).

Meditation: What are some of the inner movements that call you to life, that call you toward death? What standards and criteria do you use in making spiritual decisions?

Prayer: Holy Spirit, grant us the grace of wisdom and discernment. Our lives are complex and messy. We stand in need of your enlightenment. Guide us in the way of truth and love; give us the courage to be authentic disciples. Come, Holy Spirit, come.

January 6: Tuesday after Epiphany

Coordinates: Love and Prayer

Readings: 1 John 4:7-10; Mark 6:34-44

Scripture:
Beloved, let us love one another,
    because love is of God;
        everyone who loves is begotten by God and knows God.
            (1 John 4:7)

Reflection: The correlation between love and prayer is an interesting one. Samuel Taylor Coleridge (1772–1834) is famous for his verse "The Rime of the Ancient Mariner" (1798). In that lengthy poem, he shares an insight regarding prayer and love:

Farewell, farewell! but this I tell
To thee, thou Wedding-Guest!
He prayeth well, who loveth well
Both man and bird and beast.

He prayeth best, who loveth best
All things both great and small;
For the dear God who loveth us,
He made and loveth all. (pt. VII, ll. 611–18)

God, whose proper name is Love, made and loves all things, however great, however small. We too are called to love. The poet Coleridge claims that the best pray-er is the best lover.

And we all know that the people or communities that pray but do not share their loaves and fish with others lack authenticity. The spiritual life is a single coin that has on one side the word PRAY, and on the other LOVE!

Love and prayer are both characterized by similar attributes: attention, affirmation, admiration, appreciation, affection, adoration. The reason for this is that our relationship with God and with the human community is to be of quality and meaning, demands that we be attentive and affirming, that we admire and appreciate others, that we have affection and reverence toward all.

In his great autobiography *The Confessions*, St. Augustine offers a prayer about the topic of love, the two coordinates of our faith life: "Too late have I loved you, O Beauty, so ancient and so new, too late have I loved you" (bk. 10, chap. 27). May we have no regrets when our days on earth have ended.

Meditation: What seasons of your life have you found most prayerful, most loving? In what ways did these two activities interact?

Prayer: God of love, instill in us a deep appreciation of all creation. May our prayer life overflow into loving deeds, and may those we love be taken into the silence of our prayer. Make our spirituality real and authentic. May we share our bread and clothing with others.

January 7: Wednesday after Epiphany

Saucy Doubts and Fears

Readings: 1 John 4:11-18; Mark 6:45-52

Scripture:
There is no fear in love,
 but perfect love drives out fear
 because fear has to do with punishment,
 and so one who fears is not yet perfect in love.
  (1 John 4:18)

Reflection: There are hundreds of phobias acknowledged by psychologists, ranging from arachibutyrophobia, the fear of getting peanut butter stuck to the roof of the mouth, to phobophobia, the fear of fear itself. It seems that no one is immune, everyone fearing something.

Apparently, no one has that perfect love that drives out all fear. We live in a dangerous world and, at any moment, we can suffer injury, even death. In such a precarious environment it is difficult to trust and yet, if fear rules our lives, we can become paralyzed and miss out on existence.

Throughout the Scriptures, we keep hearing the refrain "Do not be afraid!" Isaiah the prophet says it (Isa 43:1), today's gospel says it (Mark 6:50b), the psalmist says it (Ps 118:6). What drives out fear is the experience of the loving presence of God, a God who is providential and faithful. Fear is not eradicated by self-reliance but by the presence of a merciful and loving God.

In Shakespeare's *Macbeth* we read, "But now I am cabin'd, cribb'd, confined, bound in / To saucy doubts and fears" (III, iv, ll. 24–25). Macbeth was wanting in love and his life was one of imprisonment, not by chains but by inner fears, doubts, and guilt. Only grace, the proper name of love, could free him and us from our saucy fears, our saucy doubts.

Meditation: What are the fears that hold you hostage? Why does the presence of a loving person minimize our fears? What role does the scriptural refrain "Do not be afraid" play in your spiritual life?

Prayer: Providential and faithful God, may we experience the nearness of your love and strength. So many events and so much inner turmoil cause trepidation in our hearts. Send your loving Spirit to drive out fear; give us the strength and courage to do good and to love as you have taught us. Come, Holy Spirit, come.

January 8: Thursday after Epiphany

Jesus the Pedagogue

Readings: 1 John 4:19–5:4; Luke 4:14-22a

Scripture:
Jesus returned to Galilee in the power of the Spirit,
    and news of him spread throughout the whole region.
He taught in their synagogues and was praised by all.
    (Luke 4:14-15)

Reflection: There are few vocations more important than that of being a teacher. Teachers help shape the minds, hearts, and imaginations of their students. Indeed, they are influential in shaping the destiny of those they teach. In his biography of Cardinal Newman, Ian Ker wrote, "He [Newman] has also set his face against an ecclesiastical career: the 'most useful men,' he felt, were not the leaders of the Church but its teachers, whose memory endured not so much in their writings as in the 'school of pupils who trace their moral parentage to them.'"

Jesus taught in synagogues, on hillsides, from boats, on the road. He was an agent of truth offering a vision of the meaning of life and the beauty of his Father's kingdom. And we know his message: love one another, forgive often, have compassion for the suffering and poor. He taught about repentance and conversion, about blessedness and hope, about creation and eternal life. We continue to hear his words in

Scripture and to witness his life in his deeds of love and mercy. Jesus continues to teach us through the church and the treasury of our tradition.

All this means that we are lifelong learners of our faith. We need to ponder our creed, read about the saints, study our catechisms. Our minds hunger for truth as much as our hearts thirst for love. Like Mary, we are invited to sit at Jesus' feet in prayer and, like St. Paul, discern God's presence in all things. Jesus is *the* teacher not only in words but by his life of self-sacrifice. The lessons taught by the cross and empty tomb are the foundations of our hope.

Meditation: Who are the "faith" teachers in your life? Whom do you instruct in matters of faith? Do you consider yourself a teacher (if only by your lifestyle)?

Prayer: Jesus, instruct us in your ways. Too easily we forget your wisdom and get distracted by philosophies so different from your own. May your Spirit come upon us so that we too might be agents of truth and goodness. Come, Holy Spirit, come.

January 9: Friday after Epiphany

An Internal Miracle

Readings: 1 John 5:5-13; Luke 5:12-16

Scripture:
 [A]nd when he [a man full of leprosy] saw Jesus,
 he fell prostrate, pleaded with him, and said,
 "Lord, if you wish, you can make me clean." (Luke 5:12b)

Reflection: Damien de Veuster (1840–99), better known as Damien of Molokai, asked to serve the notorious leper colony in the Hawaiian Islands. He knew full well what might happen and it did. He too contracted that dreaded disease and died of leprosy on April 15, 1899. In 1995, Pope John Paul II beatified him for his outstanding witness to the Gospel; in 2009, Pope Benedict XVI canonized Damien.

One might wonder how many people approached Father Damien to be cured, crying out, "make me clean!" Damien performed no miracle here but he gave every person a sense of dignity and worth. This *was* a miracle in its own right by his giving to the members of the leper colony an experience of God's love and care. And, one might wonder, did Damien himself ask his Lord Jesus for a cure?

As a priest Fr. Damien preached the Scripture and he knew the passage from today's first reading: "And this is the testimony: / God gave us eternal life, / and this life is in his Son" (1 John 5:11). As Damien shared the sacraments with the lepers, he was an instrument and channel of divine grace. Life flowed through his ministry as he preached and taught his people about the person of Jesus. Surely, Damien informed his people that Jesus' wish was that they be cured, if not of their disease, then of their sense of unworthiness or abandonment. For Jesus was with them in the person of Damien; for Jesus was with them as Damien died in their community.

In her poem "There's a certain Slant of light," Emily Dickinson talks about despair, a disease that rivals leprosy in its suffering. In the course of the poem she maintains that the real differences in life are internal, which is where meaning can be found. Damien performed many internal miracles as he brought hope of eternal life to his community.

Meditation: Is the distinction between internal and external miracles a valid one? Have you ever witnessed or experienced an internal miracle, a deep change in the heart and soul?

Prayer: Jesus, we all wish to be clean and pure. Send your Spirit to give us your life and love. Transform us deep within so that we might be better instruments of your grace. Our diseases are many, our anxieties so abundant. Heal us so that our energies will be directed outward in serving others rather than inward with too much self-absorption.

January 10: Saturday after Epiphany

The Best Man

Readings: 1 John 5:14-21; John 3:22-30

Scripture:
The one who has the bride is the bridegroom;
    the best man, who stands and listens for him,
    rejoices greatly at the bridegroom's voice.
So this joy of mine has been made complete. (John 3:29)

Reflection: John the Baptist possessed clarity about his mission. He was not the bridegroom at this wedding we call redemption. Rather, he prepared the way for the Redeemer and as Jesus' ministry began, John was to take a secondary role and, in fact, his mission was accomplished.

Often wedding celebrations hit a snag. The best man and the other groomsmen can get out of hand and attempt to usurp the limelight. This becomes not only inappropriate but quite embarrassing for everyone. Knowing and keeping one's place at a wedding and in life is a sign of maturity.

Not only was John the Baptist willing to "decrease" in importance as Jesus "increased," but John also took joy in recognizing the attention that people were paying to his cousin. With the coming of the Messiah, redemption was at hand. Herein lies John's joy: the salvation of the world. Though John would soon be executed at the hand of Herod, his mission was over; the kingdom of God had been furthered by his ministry.

Anwar Sadat (1918–81), the third president of Egypt who was assassinated in 1981, in his *In Search of Identity: An Autobiography*, wrote, "Nasser died without ever experiencing joie de vivre." John the Baptist was also murdered but not before experiencing the joy of living. He was the best of best men.

Meditation: Why is it so difficult to know and keep one's place in the scheme of things? When have you experienced the joy of living?

Prayer: Lord Jesus, continue to grace us with wisdom and maturity so that we might know our place in your plan of salvation. May we recognize your voice as John the Baptist did, and give you priority in our lives. As you call us to approach the wedding banquet of the Eucharist, may we be the best men and women we can be.

Heaven's Voice

Readings: Isa 42:1-4, 6-7 or Isa 55:1-11; Acts 10:34-38 or
1 John 5:1-9; Mark 1:7-11

Scripture:
And a voice came from the heavens,
"You are my beloved Son; with you I am well pleased."
  (Mark 1:11)

Reflection: Baptism is about relationships. We are baptized
into a community of faith; we are baptized into the life of
God; we are baptized into a life of discipleship to Jesus. And
yes, we are baptized through the power of the Holy Spirit.

Relationships demand communication. In the spiritual life
that form of communication is called prayer, be it a prayer
of praise, gratitude, petition, or forgiveness. Prayer is that
lifting up of our minds, hearts, and lives to a loving God
who calls each of us beloved. Today as we hear about Jesus
being baptized, we are also informed that following that
experience he was in prayer. Jesus heard the Father's voice
that he was the beloved Son.

Jesus prayed at the Jordan River. Here he experienced the
identity of being God's beloved Son. How important that
was for him because sometime later, while hanging on the
cross, he would be challenged to come down "if" he was
truly the Son of God. The grace of baptism sustained him in
this moment of anguish.

Jesus prayed in deserted places. He sought solitude to communicate with his Father. It was out of this prayer that he would teach, preach, and heal. It would be out of this prayer that he would discern the choice of apostles.

Jesus prayed in a garden, the one called Gethsemane. In the sorrowful mysteries of the rosary, we call this mystery "the agony in the garden." Just as Jesus experienced the death/resurrection mystery of his baptism at the Jordan, so now again he came to experience that dying/rising event that would lead to our salvation.

Baptism takes place in a moment of time but it is also a permanent invitation to nurture and foster our spiritual relationships. As we celebrate Jesus' baptism, let us renew our own.

Meditation: In what sense is baptism a permanent invitation? What role does prayer play in your spiritual life?

Prayer: Lord Jesus, draw us more deeply into the mystery of your life. May our understanding of our baptisms inspire us to prayer and, yes, good works. Teach us once again how to pray; teach us once again the way of discipleship. May your Holy Spirit descend upon us and may we too hear that we are your Father's beloved children.

References

Introduction
Austin Flannery, OP, *Vatican Council II: The Basic Sixteen Documents* (Collegeville, MN: Liturgical Press, 2014).

John XXIII, Message to Humanity, October 20, 1962, in *The Documents of Vatican II*, ed. Walter M. Abbot (New York: Herder and Herder, 1966), 3–4.

December 3: Saint Francis Xavier, Priest
Alan Paton, *Towards the Mountain* (New York: Charles Scribner's Sons, 1980), 232.

December 4: Thursday of the First Week of Advent
"Editor's Odyssey: Gleanings from Articles and Editorials by N.C.," *Saturday Review* (April 15, 1978): 13.

December 5: Friday of the First Week of Advent
Flannery O'Connor, *The Habit of Being: Letters of Flannery O'Connor*, ed. Sally Fitzgerald (New York: Farrar, Straus and Giroux, 1988), 354.

December 6: Saturday of the First Week of Advent
Jim Wallis, *The Call to Conversion* (San Francisco: Harper & Row, 1981), 53.

December 7: Second Sunday of Advent
Jean Sulivan, *Eternity, My Beloved* (St. Paul, MN: River Boats Books, 1966), 10.

December 9: Tuesday of the Second Week of Advent
Francis Thompson, "The Hound of Heaven" (1893).
Romano Guardini, *The Lord* (Chicago: Henry Regnery, 1954), 424.

December 10: Wednesday of the Second Week of Advent
Teresa of Avila, *The Way of Perfection*, in *St. Teresa of Avila: Volume Two, The Complete Works* (London: Continuum, 2002), 98.

December 11: Thursday of the Second Week of Advent
Dave Kindred, *Sound and Fury: Two Powerful Lives, One Fateful Friendship* (New York: Free Press, 2006), 58.
Aelred Squire, *Asking the Fathers* (Westminster, MD: Christian Classics, 1993), 217.

December 13: Saint Lucy, Virgin and Martyr
Francis de Sales, *Introduction to the Devout Life*, ed. and trans. Allan Ross (Mineola, NY: Dover, 2009), 178.

December 14: Third Sunday of Advent
Walter Brueggemann, *The Bible Makes Sense* (Winona, MN: St. Mary's College Press, 1977), 88.

December 15: Monday of the Third Week of Advent
John Henry Cardinal Newman, *Apologia Pro Vita Sua*, ed. Frank M. Turner (New Haven, CT: Yale University Press, 2008), 363.

December 16: Tuesday of the Third Week of Advent
John Henry Cardinal Newman, *An Essay on the Development of Christian Doctrine* (Notre Dame, IN: University of Notre Dame Press, 1989), chap. 1, section I.7.

December 18: Thursday in Late Advent
Office of Readings, Evening Prayer, *The Liturgy of the Hours*, vol. I (New York: Catholic Book Publishing, 1975), 333.

December 20: Saturday in Late Advent
Louis-Marie Chauvet, *The Sacraments: The Word of God at the Mercy of the Body* (Collegeville, MN: Liturgical Press, 2001), 83.

December 21: Fourth Sunday of Advent
Anne Morrow Lindbergh, *Gift from the Sea* (New York: Random House, 2005), 44.

December 23: Tuesday in Late Advent
John Henry Cardinal Newman, *Apologia Pro Vita Sua*, ed. Frank M. Turner (New Haven, CT: Yale University Press, 2008), 305.

December 24: Wednesday in Late Advent (Christmas Eve)
Douglas Steere, *Together in Solitude* (New York: Crossroad, 1982), 188.
William James, *The Varieties of Religious Experience* (New York: Modern Library, 1936), 350.

December 26: Saint Stephen, First Martyr
Yves Congar, *I Believe in the Holy Spirit*, vol. 2 (New York: Crossroad, 1997), 9, 8.

December 27: Saint John, Apostle and Evangelist
Emily Dickinson, "This World is not conclusion," in *Dickinson: Selected Poems and Commentaries*, Helen Vendler, 173 (Cambridge, MA: Belknap Press of Harvard University Press, 2010).

December 30: Sixth Day in the Octave of Christmas
Thornton Wilder, *Our Town: A Play in Three Acts* (New York: Coward-McCann, 1965), 83.

December 31: Seventh Day in the Octave of Christmas
Cardinal Carlo Maria Martini, *The Joy of the Gospel: Meditations for Young People*, trans. James McGrath (Collegeville, MN: Liturgical Press, 1994), 37.

January 2: Saints Basil the Great and Gregory Nazianzen, Bishops and Doctors of the Church
Flannery O'Connor, *The Habit of Being: Letters of Flannery O'Connor*, ed. Sally Fitzgerald (New York: Farrar, Straus and Giroux, 1979), 453.

Jessica Powers, "The Master Beggar," in *The Selected Poetry of Jessica Powers* (Washington, DC: ICS Publications, 1999), 23. © 1999, 1984 Carmelite Monastery, Pewaukee, WI. Used with permission.

January 4: The Epiphany of the Lord
C. S. Lewis, *The Magician's Nephew*, ill. by Pauline Baynes (New York: Scholastic, 1995), 136.

January 5: Monday after Epiphany
Jon Sobrino, *Christology at the Crossroads: A Latin American Approach*, trans. John Drury (Maryknoll, NY: Orbis, 1978), 129.

January 8: Thursday after Epiphany
Ian Ker, *John Henry Newman: A Biography* (New York: Oxford University Press, 1988), 42.

January 9: Friday after Epiphany
Emily Dickinson, "There's a certain Slant of light," in *Dickinson: Selected Poems and Commentaries*, Helen Vendler, 126 (Cambridge, MA: Belknap Press of Harvard University Press, 2010).

January 10: Saturday after Epiphany
Anwar Sadat, *In Search of Identity: An Autobiography* (New York: Harper & Row, 1978), 78.